GW00501318

OWN GOALS!

The world's funniest football quotes

Crombie Jardine
Publishing Limited
Office 2
3 Edgar Buildings
George Street
Bath
BA1 2FJ
www.crombiejardine.com

ISBN: 978-1-906051-42-6

Published by Crombie Jardine Publishing Limited, 2010

Compiled by Crombie Jardine Publishing Limited

Printed and bound in China

Contents

Introduction

"Some people believe football is a matter of life and death. I am very disappointed with that attitude. I can assure you it is much, much more important than that"

This quote by the late, great Bill Shankly is perhaps the best to sum up what football means to many millions of people around the world.

Own Goals! is a collection of the world's funniest quotations from commentators, managers and players.

Some of you might be critical that most of the quotes are British and you would have a good point! But let's be clear about this: we invented this game and we think that quite honestly our pundits are the best and funniest in the world!

If you have any quotes you would like to see
in a future edition, please email them to
catriona@crombiejardine.com

A

"Strangely, in slow motion replay, the ball seemed to hang in the air for even longer"
David Acfield

"It looks as if I am trying to stab Dave Bassett in the back but I'm not holding a gun to anybody's head"
Mickey Adams

"Defoe's cramp might come from drinking caffeine. I used to get cramp because I put 20 pints of lager down my neck"
Tony Adams

"Fergie said I was a Manchester United player in the wrong shirt. I said he was an Arsenal manager in the wrong blazer"
Tony Adams

"I'd rather not talk to anyone and just go and walk my chickens"
Tony Adams

"Last night, we were the best team on the day"
Roy Aitken

"If Ricardo Gardner should have been sent off, there should have been four players sent off for each side. So the match should have ended up six against six"
Sam Allardyce

"A lot of hard work went into this defeat"
Malcolm Allison

"It's not true. Technically you can say it's true, yes"
Steve Archibald

"We have been saying this, both pre-season and before the season started"
Len Ashurst

Ron Atkinson (b.1939)

Media commentator and former football player and manager.

Known as "Big Ron". Ronald Franklin Atkinson was born in Liverpool, England, on 18 March 1939.

He played for Oxford United before managing such teams as Cambridge United, West Bromwich Albion, Manchester United, Aston Villa and Nottingham Forest. He led Manchester United to FA Cup victory in 1983 and 1985.

As a media commentator, he become one of Britain's best-known football pundits and his remarks have become known as "Big-Ronisms" or "Ronglish".

He courted controversy in 2004 when, believing his microphone to be off whilst commentating for ITV Sport, he made a racist remark about a player. He regretted his error of judgment immediately and offered his resignation, which was accepted.

$\sim$

"At international level, giving the ball away
doesn't work too often"
Ron Atkinson

"Beckenbauer really has gambled all his eggs"
Ron Atkinson

"He actually looks a little twat, that Totti"
Ron Atkinson

"He is without doubt the greatest sweeper in
the world, I'd say, at a guess"
Ron Atkinson

"His white boots were on fire against Arsenal,
and he'll be looking for them to reproduce
tonight"
Ron Atkinson

"If Glenn Hoddle said one word to his team at
half time, it was 'concentration' and 'focus'"
Ron Atkinson

"I know where he should have put his flag up,
and he'd have got plenty of help"
Ron Atkinson

"I'm going to make a prediction – it could go
either way"
Ron Atkinson

"I never comment on referees and I'm not going
to break the habit of a lifetime for that prat"
Ron Atkinson

"I think that was a moment of cool panic there"
Ron Atkinson

"I would also think that the action replay showed it to be worse than it actually was"
Ron Atkinson

"I would not say he [David Ginola] is the best left winger in the Premiership, but there are none better"
Ron Atkinson

"That boy throws a ball further than I go on holiday"
Ron Atkinson on Dave Challinor of Tranmere

"The keeper should have saved that one but he did"
Ron Atkinson

"The Spaniards have been reduced to aiming aimless balls into the box"
Ron Atkinson

B

"And I honestly believe we can go all the way to
Wembley unless somebody knocks us out"
Dave Bassett

"It's been two ends of the same coin"
Dave Bassett

"It would be foolish to believe that automatic
promotion is automatic in any way whatsoever"
Dave Bassett

"Obviously for Scunthorpe it would be a nice
scalp to put Wimbledon on their bottoms"
Dave Bassett

"The past is history"
Dave Bassett

"You have got to miss them to score sometimes"
Dave Bassett

"You weigh up the pros and cons and try to put
them into chronological order"
Dave Bassett

"I don't believe in luck... but I do believe
you need it"
Alan Ball

"The important thing is he shook hands with us
over the phone"
Alan Ball

"I just felt that the whole night, the conditions
and taking everything into consideration and
everything being equal, and everything is equal,
we should have got something from the game –
but we didn't"
John Barnes

"We are a good average team"
Franz Beckenbauer

David Beckham (b.1975)

Footballer.

Known as "Becks". David Robert Joseph Beckham was born in London, England, on 2 May 1975.

He has played for Manchester United, Real Madrid, Los Angeles Galaxy, AC Milan and the England national team.

He was the first British footballer to play 100 Champions League matches.

He was inducted into England's National Football Museum's Hall of Fame in 2008.

Beckham is also a fashion icon, 'metrosexual', advertising agent's dream, endorser of Armani men's underwear, Gillette and Adidas... BBC Sports Personality of the year in 2001, tattoo-lover, man of many hairdos, supporter of UNICEF...

$\sim$

"Alex Ferguson is the best manager I've ever had at this level. Well, he's the only manager I've actually had at this level. But he's the best manager I've ever had"
David Beckham

"I remember so clearly us going into hospital so Victoria could have Brooklyn. I was eating a Lion bar at the time"
David Beckham

"My parents have been there for me, ever since I was about seven"
David Beckham

"Pelé was a complete player. I didn't see him live obviously, because I wasn't born"
David Beckham

"We're definitely going to get Brooklyn christened, but we don't know into which religion"
David Beckham

"Well, I can play in the centre, on the right and occasionally on the left side"
David Beckham, when asked if he thought that he was a volatile player

"He [Souness] has just gone behind my back in front of my face"
Craig Bellamy

"It wasn't the greatest pitch and there was no atmosphere. No excuses though"
Craig Bellamy

"My team-mates advised me to visit the city first. I went to have a look at Middlesbrough and decided I was better off in Parma"
Antonio Bennarivo

"I spent a lot of money on booze, birds and fast cars. The rest I just squandered"
George Best

Own Goals!

"It's tight. Just how I like them"
Gary Birtles

"I once threw my shirt to the fans in the crowd
and they threw it back!"
George Boateng

"I promise results, not promises"
John Bond

"Apart from the fact that we couldn't defend
properly and we couldn't attack properly, what
was wrong with us?"
Adrian Boothroyd

"I know what my strengths are, and I know what
my not strengths are"
Adrian Boothroyd

"I have a curiosity over Beckham. I want to see
if he is equipped as he is in the Armani
underwear ads"
Marco Borrielllo

"An agent recommended a 14-year-old, but there
was something strange about him, apart from
the beard and receding hairline"
Karren Brady

"Footballers are only interested in drinking,
clothes, and the size of their willies"
Karren Brady

"If Sunderland's so great, why doesn't Roy Keane
live there instead of flying in from his home in
Cheshire by helicopter every morning?"
Karren Brady

"That's football, Mike. Northern Ireland have had several chances and haven't scored but England have had no chances and scored twice"
Trevor Brooking

"Soccer is the biggest thing that's happened in creation. It's bigger than any 'ism' you can name"
Alan Brown

"I strongly feel that the only difference between the two teams were the goals that England scored"
Craig Brown

"It is now fashionable for expectant fathers to be with their wives at the birth"
Craig Brown

"Michael Owen – he's got the legs of a salmon"
Craig Brown

"The underdogs will start favourites for
this match"
Craig Brown

"They had a dozen corners, maybe twelve
– I'm guessing"
Craig Brown

"My smile is forced. It's actually wind"
Phil Brown

"We didn't look like scoring, although we looked
like we were going to get a goal"
Alan Buckley

"Five days shalt thou labour, as the Bible says.
The seventh day is the Lord thy God's. The sixth
day is for football"
Anthony Burgess

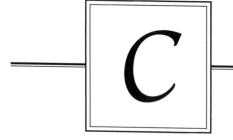

"The man who comes to take care of my piranhas told me that if I left West Ham he would kill all my fish!"
Paolo di Canio

"I am searching for abstract ways of expressing reality, abstract forms that will enlighten my own mystery"
Eric Cantona

"When the seagulls follow the trawler, it is because they think sardines will be thrown into the sea"
Eric Cantona

"There's a rat in the camp trying to throw a spanner into the works"
Chris Cattlin

"Some people tell me that we professional players are soccer slaves. Well, if this is slavery, give me a life sentence"
Bobby Charlton

"If in winning we only draw we would be fine"
Jack Charlton

"It was a game we should have won. We lost it
because we thought we were going to win it.
But then again, I thought that there was no way
we were going to get a result there"
Jack Charlton

"I've seen them on television on a Sunday
morning most days of the week"
Jack Charlton

"We probably got on better with the likes of
Holland, Belgium, Norway and Sweden, some of
whom are not even European"
Jack Charlton

"This is an unusual Scotland side because they
have good players"
Javier Clemente

Brian Clough (1935-2004)

Footballer and manager.

Known as "Cloughie". Brian Howard Clough was born on 21 March 1935 in Middlesbrough, England, and died in Derby, England, on 20 September 2004, from stomach cancer.

After having played for Middlesbrough and Sunderland, and the England national team, Brian Clough managed Hartlepool United, Derby County, Brighton & Hove Albion, Leeds United and Nottingham Forest.

Both popular and outspoken, he will be remembered as one of the greatest managers of the English game. Ironically, though, he never managed the England team.

On being asked his attitude towards the England selectors (when he did not get the job) he replied, "I'm sure the England selectors thought if they took me on and gave me the job, I'd want to run the show. They were shrewd because that's exactly what I would have done."

His autobiography is *Cloughie: Walking on Water. My Life*. His strong views on football issues were often aired in a column he wrote for *Four Four Two* magazine up until his death.

He was inducted into England's National Football Museum's Hall of Fame in 2002 and into the special European Hall of Fame in 2008.

When awarded an OBE in 1991, he responded by saying that it stood for Old Big 'Ead.

On being remembered, he said, "I want no epitaphs of profound history and all that type of thing. I contributed. I would hope they would say that, and I would hope somebody liked me" and "Don't send me flowers when I'm dead, send them to me now if you like me."

His memorial service was held at Derby's Pride Park Stadium and was attended by over 14,000 people.

~

"Beckham? His wife can't sing and his barber
can't cut hair"
Brian Clough

"He should guide Posh in the direction of a
singing coach because she's nowhere near as
good at her job as her husband"
Brian Clough's advice for David Beckham

"If a chairman sacks a manager that he initially
appointed, then he should go as well"
Brian Clough

"If a player had said to Bill Shankly 'I've got to
speak to my agent', Bill would have hit him. And I
would have held him while he hit him"
Brian Clough

"If God had intended for us to play football in
the clouds he would have put grass up there"
Brian Clough referring to the long ball game

"I like my women to be feminine, not sliding into
tackles and covered in mud"
Brian Clough

"I only ever hit Roy [Keane] the once. He got up
so I couldn't have hit him very hard"
Brian Clough

"I wouldn't say I was the best manager in the
business. But I was in the top one"
Brian Clough

"Walk on water? I know most people out there
will be saying that instead of walking on it, I
should have taken more of it with my drinks.
They are absolutely right"
Brian Clough

"On occasions I have been big-headed. I think most
people are when they get in the limelight. I call
myself Big 'Ead just to remind myself not to be"
Brian Clough

"Players lose you games, not tactics. There's so much crap talked about tactics by people who barely know how to win at dominoes"
Brian Clough

"That Seaman is a handsome young man but he spends too much time looking in his mirror rather than at the ball. You can't keep goal with hair like that"
Brian Clough

"The river Trent is lovely, I know because I have walked on it for eighteen years"
Brian Clough

"They say Rome wasn't built in a day, but I wasn't on that particular job"
Brian Clough

"We talk about it for twenty minutes and then we decide I was right"
Brian Clough on dealing with disruptive players

"I'm not going to make it a target but it's
something to aim for"
Steve Coppell

"Referees don't come down here with a
particular flavoured shirt on"
Steve Coppell

"The lad got over-excited when he saw the
whites of the goalpost's eyes"
Steve Coppell

"There isn't a lot going on in this match. The two
teams have just been playing against each
other"
Tony Cottee

"International football's about getting players to
come at the same time"
Steve Cotterill

Own Goals!

"I am absolutely delighted to get back into football with Livingston"
Kenny Dalglish

"As I've said before and I've said in the past..."
Kenny Dalglish

"And with just four minutes gone, the score is already 0-0"
Ian Dark

"I'm not saying I'm going or I'm not going. But maybe tomorrow I'm not here"
El-Hadji Diouf

"Chester made it hard for us by having two players sent off"
John Docherty

"I would have to be deaf not to read the allegations"
Bobby Downes

"Everyone knows what happens now, but
nobody knows"
Sven Goran Eriksson

"Football is much harder if you don't have
the ball"
Sven Goran Eriksson

"We need goals when the score line is 0-0"
Sven Goran Eriksson

Richard Keys : "Well, Roy, do you think that
you'll have to finish above Manchester United to
win the league?"
Roy Evans : "You have to finish above everyone
to win the league, Richard"

Alex Ferguson (b.1941)

Football manager and former player.

Known as "Sir Alex" and "Fergie". Alexander Chapman Ferguson was born in Glasgow, Scotland, on 31 December 1941.

As a player his clubs were Queen's Park, St. Johnstone, Dunfermline Athletic, Rangers, Falkirk and Ayr United.

As a manager, his clubs have been East Stirlingshire, St. Mirren, Aberdeen, the Scotland national team and Manchester United. He was appointed manager of Manchester United in November 1986 and is the second-longest serving manager in their history after Sir Matt Busby. At the club, he has guided the team to 11 League Championships and two Champions League titles.

He is now one of the most successful managers in football history.

In 1999, he became the first manager to lead an English team to win the treble of League

Championship, FA Cup and UEFA Champions League. As well as being the only manager to win the FA Cup five times, he is also the only manager in history to win three successive League Championships in the top flight in England with the same club (1999, 2000 and 2001, and again in 2007, 2008 and 2009).

He was inducted into England's National Football Museum's Hall of Fame in 2002, inducted into the special European Hall of Fame in 2008, was knighted in 1999, and holds the Freedom of the City of Aberdeen for his services to the city, having managed the city's football club to a host of major trophies in the early to mid 1980s. He was awarded a CBE (1994-95) and an OBE (1982-83).

$\sim$

Own Goals!

"As with every young player, he's only eighteen"
Alex Ferguson

"Cole should be scoring from those distances, but I'm not going to single him out"
Alex Ferguson

"It's a conflict of parallels"
Alex Ferguson

"It was particularly pleasing that our goal scorers scored tonight"
Alex Ferguson

"The lads ran their socks into the ground"
Alex Ferguson

"The philosophy of a lot of European teams, even in home matches, is not to give a goal away"
Alex Ferguson

"They'll miss the physical presence of Van Hennegor, or whatever ye call him... him from Castlemilk"
Alex Ferguson

"This pilot move by FIFA will take root and fly"
Alex Ferguson

"Players win games and players lose games. It's all about players really"
Bobby Ferguson

"Dumbarton player Steve McCahill has limped off with a badly cut forehead"
Tom Ferrie

"If you had to name one particular person to blame it would have to be one of the players"
Theo Foley

Own Goals!

"Systems are made by players rather than
players making systems"
Theo Foley

"The dice are stacked against them"
Theo Foley

"It would have killed them off a little bit"
Gerry Francis

"Klinsmann has taken to English football like a
duck out of water"
Gerry Francis

"What I said to them at half time would be
unprintable on the radio"
Gerry Francis

G

Own Goals!

"I never make predictions, and I never will"
Paul Gascoigne

"It was a big relief off my shoulder"
Paul Gascoigne

"I've had fourteen bookings this season
– eight of which were my fault, but seven of
which were disputable"
Paul Gascoigne

"Two Andy Gorams, there's only two Andy Gorams"
*Kilmarnock fans to the Rangers keeper after he
had been diagnosed with mild schizophrenia*

"Give him his head and he'll take it with both
hands or feet"
Bobby Gould

"It's thrown a spanner in the fire"
Bobby Gould

"The one thing I didn't expect is the way we didn't play"
George Graham

"They haven't lived up to the expectations we expect of them"
George Graham

"Carvalho is one of those defenders who defends"
Andy Gray

"I was saying the other day how often the most vulnerable area, for goalies, is between their legs"
Andy Gray

"We signed to play until the day we died, and we did"
Jimmy Greaves

"It was that game that put the Everton ship back on the road"
Alan Green

Own Goals!

"Mido goes down clutching his right head"
Alan Green

"Being given chances, and not taking them.
That's what life is all about"
Ron Greenwood

"Bryan Robson, well, he does what he does and
his future is in the future"
Ron Greenwood

"Glenn Hoddle hasn't been the Hoddle we know.
Neither has Bryan Robson"
Ron Greenwood

"In comparison, there's no comparison"
Ron Greenwood

"To me personally, it's nothing personal to me"
Ron Greenwood

"Playing with wingers is more effective against European sides like Brazil than English sides like Wales"
Ron Greenwood

"He's gone in there with studs up and has cut someone in half, but I don't want to criticise him"
John Gregory

"Back in my day, Carlo Ancelotti never smoked at all. Or maybe he did"
Ruud Gullit

"We must have had 99% of the game. It was the other 3% that cost us the match"
Ruud Gullit

"You know what they say: If it ain't Dutch, it ain't much"
Ruud Gullit

"Failure happens all the time. It happens every day in practice. What makes you better is how you react to it"
Mia Hamm

"The person that said winning isn't everything never won anything"
Mia Hamm

"I don't think anyone enjoyed it. Apart from the people who watched it"
Alan Hansen

"Kuyt allowed Keane to come inside him"
Alan Hansen

"Guus Hiddink's good at feeling players"
Jimmy Floyd Hasselbaink

Glenn Hoddle (b.1957)

Football manager and former player.

Glenn Hoddle was born in Hayes, England, on 27 October 1957.

He played for Tottenham Hotspur, AS Monaco, Swindon Town and Chelsea, as well as for the England national team before managing such teams as Chelsea, England, Southampton and Tottenham Hotspur.

In 2007 he was inducted into England's National Football Museum's Hall of Fame.

Respected by fans and players, Hoddle has not always enjoyed such a good relationship with the press.

"He's a good footballer with a bit of everything
and certainly two good feet – which is unusual
these days"
Glenn Hoddle

"His tackle was definitely pre-ordained"
Glenn Hoddle

"I have a number of alternatives, and each one
gives me something different"
Glenn Hoddle

"I think in international football you have to be
able to handle the ball"
Glenn Hoddle

"Michael Owen is a goal scorer – not a natural
born one, not yet. That takes time"
Glenn Hoddle

"Okay, so we lost, but good things can come
from it – negative and positive"
Glenn Hoddle

"Robert Lee was able to do some running on his
groin for the first time"
Glenn Hoddle

"75% of what happens to Paul Gascoigne in his
life is fiction"
Glenn Hoddle

"Steven Carr has hit a small blimp"
Glenn Hoddle

"The minute's silence was immaculate, I have
never heard a minute's silence like that"
Glenn Hoddle

"When a player gets to thirty, so does his body"
Glenn Hoddle

"With hindsight, it's easy to look at it
with hindsight"
Glenn Hoddle

"You can't go to sleep on Berbatov, he'll get
behind you and open you up"
Glenn Hoddle

"The only way we will be going to Europe
is if the club splash out and take us all to
Eurodisney"
Dean Holdsworth

"A contract on a piece of paper, saying you
want to leave, is like a piece of paper saying you
want to leave"
John Hollins

Own Goals!

"I don't like it when they call me 'madcap'. I'm not mad and I don't wear a cap"
Ian Holloway

"To be talking about vital games at this stage of the season is ridiculous, really, but tomorrow's game is absolutely vital"
Brian Horton

"At the end of the day, the Arsenal fans demand that we put eleven players on the pitch"
Don Howe

"They'll perhaps finish in the top three. I can't see them going any higher"
Don Howe

"We've got Chester and Grimsby next. You can't get any bigger than that"
Eddie Howe

1

Own Goals!

"And the score is nil-nil, just as it was at the
beginning of the game"
Mike Ingham

"Martin O'Neill, standing, hands on hips,
stroking his chin"
Mike Ingham

"The Uruguayans are losing no time in making a
meal around the referee"
Mike Ingham

"Tottenham are trying tonight to become the
first London team to win this Cup. The last team
to do so was the 1973 Spurs side"
Mike Ingham

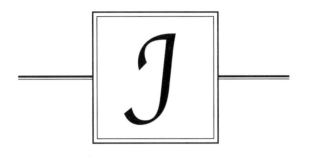

"A few years ago, Iain Dowie came with a surge"
Paul Jewell

"It was easily the happiest day of my football
life and yet people still want to ask me about
the suit. When they talk about the day,
it's not 'Didn't you do well?', it's 'What was that
you were wearing?!'"
*Paul Jewell on the day he took Bradford
to the Premiership*

"I was shocked when I was first introduced
to the fans because they brought out
a sheep, cut its head off and then smeared
blood over my forehead"
Ronnie Johnsen on life with Besiktas, Turkey

"He's one of those footballers whose brains are
in his head"
Derek Johnstone

"The new West Stand casts a giant shadow over the entire pitch, even on a sunny day"
Chris Jones

"I don't read everything I read in the press"
Dave Jones

"Overall I think we dominated for 75% of the game, but we have to make sure we do that for the other 15"
Dave Jones

"And Arsenal now have plenty of time to dictate the last few seconds"
Peter Jones

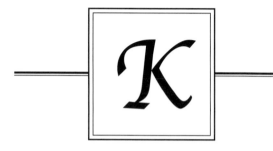

"Jimmy Bullard had two free kicks. He scored one, nearly scored from one and missed one"
Chris Kamara

"You can only bring in kids from a certain radius and a lot of our radius is in the water. Any good fish out there?"
Roy Keane

"Hull have lost three in a row. If they lose this one it'll be four in a row"
Richard Keys

"We rode our luck, but that's what the goalposts are there for"
Joe Kinnear

Kevin Keegan (b.1951)

Football manager and former player.

Joseph Kevin Keegan was born in Armthorpe, Doncaster, England, on 14 February 1951.

He played for Scunthorpe United, Liverpool, Hamburger SV, Southampton, Newcastle United and the England national team before managing Newcastle United, Fulham, England and Manchester City.

FWA Footballer of the Year 1978, European Footballer of the Year 1978, European Footballer of the Year 1979, OBE, 1982. He was inducted into England's National Football Museum's Hall of Fame in 2002 and the special European Hall of Fame in 2008.

Renowned for his 'poodle perm' in the 1970s, Keegan advertised Brut aftershave alongside Henry Cooper, released a single in 1979 called *Head Over Heels in Love* and is known for his charity appearances for the Lord's Taverners.

"At the Argentina game, how would you have guessed that Darren Anderton would have gone off with cramp?"
Kevin Keegan

"Despite his white boots, he has pace and aggression"
Kevin Keegan

"England have the best fans in the world and Scotland's fans are second to none"
Kevin Keegan

"I don't think there is anybody bigger or smaller than Maradona"
Kevin Keegan

"It was still moving when it hit the back of the net"
Kevin Keegan

"Louis Figo is different to David Beckham, and vice versa"
Kevin Keegan

"The good news for Nigeria is that they're 2-0 down very early in the game"
Kevin Keegan

"The tide is very much in our court now"
Kevin Keegan

"They compare Steve McManaman to Steve Highway and he's nothing like him, but I can see why – it's because he's a bit different"
Kevin Keegan

"They're the second best team in the world, and there's no higher praise than that"
Kevin Keegan

"My own autobiography, which was written by
Ian Ross..."
Howard Kendall

"Some of our players have got no brains, so I've
given them the day off tomorrow to rest them"
David Kemp

"For Portsmouth, Boo Boppa Diop is suspended.
Sorry, I was thinking of Bee-Bop-A-Lula"
Richard Keys

"We pressed the self-destruct button ourselves"
Brian Kidd

"I don't know what it's like out there, but it's like
an ice rink out there"
Andy Kilner

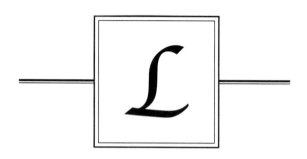

"Our first goal was pure textile"
John Lambie

"That's great. Tell him he's Pelé and get him back on"
John Lambie, when told a concussed striker did not know who he was

"If my players want to piss off England, they need to understand that the English eat badly and their women don't wash their genitalia"
Aurelio de Laurentis

"It was one of those goals that's invariably a goal"
Denis Law

"There's no way Ryan Giggs is another George Best. He's another Ryan Giggs"
Denis Law

Own Goals!

"Whoever wins today will win the championship
no matter who wins"
Denis Law

"What he's got is legs, which the other
midfielders don't have"
Lennie Lawrence

"Italy would've been better playing Swiss Toni
rather than Luca Toni"
Mark Lawrenson

"We pulled the self-destruct button"
Colin Lee

"Even when you're dead, you must never allow
yourself just to lie down and be buried"
Gordon Lee

The world's funniest football quotes

"There's no in between – you're either good or bad. We were in between"
Gary Lineker

"He's such an honest person it's untrue"
Brian Little

"Germany are a very difficult team to play... they have eleven internationals out there today"
Steve Lomas

"In terms of the Richter scale, this defeat was a force eight gale"
John Lyall

"If there weren't such a thing as football, we'd all be frustrated footballers"
Mick Lyons

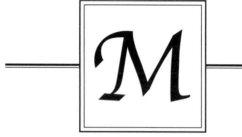

"We ended up playing football, and that's not
our style"
Alex MacDonald

"That was a great chance for Spartak's Mozart,
but he just lacked composure"
Malkie Mackay

"Working with thirty players every day, you can
only pick eleven players. So you have to deal
with the other twelve"
Gary McAllister

"It was the perfect penalty – apart from he
missed it"
Rob McCaffrey

"To be second with one game to go – you can't
ask for more"
Stuart McCall

"I can't wait for the Premier League. Win four
games before Christmas before getting sacked
at Christmas and then go on holiday"
Mick McCarthy

"Inter have bought the finished article and
there's no doubt he can keep improving"
Mick McCarthy

"It was a crap start. It was f*cking rubbish,
absolute tosh, drivel. Shite. Bullshit. Apart from
that I'm pleased"
Mick McCarthy

"I was feeling as sick as the proverbial donkey"
Mick McCarthy

"No regrets, none at all. My only regret is that we
went out on penalties. That's my only regret. But
no, no regrets"
Mick McCarthy

"If the defender had made contact and
the attacker had gone down, it would have
been a penalty"
Steve McClaren

"We are offered players every single day. We get
five or six a week"
John McClelland

"No-one hands you cups on a plate"
Terry McDermott

"Dave has this incredible knack of pulling a
couple of chickens out of the hat each season"
Mark McGhee

"I am manager of Macclesfield and am
giving the job my total commitment.
Obviously, as an Irishman, I want the job as
their international manager"
Sammy McIlroy

Own Goals!

"If Chelsea are lucky today, then I don't think
they'll be lucky"
Alan McInally

"I'm definitely maybe going to play Sturrock"
Jim McLean

"Tore's got a groin strain and he's been
playing with it"
Alex McLeish

"When you're 4-0 up you should never lose 7-1"
Laurie McMenemy

"Outside of quality we had other qualities"
Bertie Mee

"Eboue only took a penalty last week because
Arsenal were winning 28-0"
Paul Merson

"Everton are back to winning every game 1-0.
Though they won 3-0 the other week"
Paul Merson

"QPR have spent £250,000. I've gone more than
that at Coral's"
Paul Merson

"Stoke made lots of chances but not lots
of chances"
Paul Merson

"Villa have got a real chance to solidate"
Paul Merson

"Wilkins, with an inch perfect pass to no-one
in particular"
Brian Moore

John Motson (b.1945)

Football commentator and writer.

Known as "Motty". John Walker Motson was born in Manchester, England, on 10 July 1945.

His career began as a reporter for the *Barnet Press* and the *Sheffield Morning Telegraph*. He was hired as a sports presenter for BBC Radio 2 in 1968.

Since 1979 he has commentated on all the major championships: World Cups, FA Cups, and European Championships.

He was commentating on the FA Cup semi-final of 1989 between Liverpool and Nottingham Forest when the Hillsborough disaster occurred. Motson found himself commentating on a tragedy rather than a football match, and he would later appear as part of the Hillsborough enquiry, since he had been a witness.

In 1996, Motson's book, *Motty's Diary: A Year In The Life Of A Commentator* was published. Two years later, BBC 1 gave him his own TV programme, *The Full Motty*.

In 2006, he featured in the Aardman Animations movie *Flushed Away*, playing the part of the football commentator.

In 2007 he appeared on the BBC Radio 4 biographical programme *Great Lives* and he nominated Brian Clough as his 'great life'.

John Motson is famed for his sheepskin coat, which, on the satirical quiz show *They Think It's All Over,* he revealed that he bought off a man in Hornchurch along with seven identical coats, hoping that they would span his career.

In 2008, following the BBC's loss of rights to cover live football he announced his retirement from live television commentary. The Euro 2008 final was his last live TV broadcast.

≈

"And I suppose they [Spurs] are nearer to being out of the FA Cup now than at any other time since the first half of this season, when they weren't ever in it anyway"
John Motson

"And Seaman, just like a falling oak, manages to change direction"
John Motson

"And what a time to score. Twenty-two minutes gone"
John Motson

"Brazil – they're so good it's like they are running round the pitch playing with themselves"
John Motson

"Bruce has got the taste of Wembley in his nostrils"
John Motson

"For those of you watching in black and white,
Spurs are in the all yellow strip"
John Motson

"I can't fault Mark Palios too highly"
John Motson

"In a sense it's a one-man show... except there
are two men involved, Hartson and Berkovic, and
a third man, the goalkeeper"
John Motson

"I think this could be our best victory over
Germany since the war"
John Motson

"It's a football stadium in the truest sense of
the word"
John Motson

Own Goals!

"It's Arsenal 0 – Everton 1, and the longer it stays like that the more you've got to fancy Everton"
John Motson

"I was about to say, before something far more interesting interrupted..."
John Motson

"Middlesbrough are withdrawing Maccarone the Italian, Nemeth the Slovakian and Stockdale the right back"
John Motson

"Nearly all the Brazilian supporters are wearing yellow shirts – it's a fabulous kaleidoscope of colour"
John Motson

"Northern Ireland were in white, which was quite appropriate because three inches of snow had to be cleared from the pitch before kick off"
John Motson

"Not the first half you might have expected, even though the score might suggest that it was"
John Motson

"So different from the scenes in 1872, at the cup final none of us can remember"
John Motson

"That shot might not have been as good as it might have been"
John Motson

"The match has become quite unpredictable, but it still looks as though Arsenal will win the cup"
John Motson

José Mourinho (b.1963)

Football manager.

Nicknamed "The Special One". José Mário dos Santos Félix Mourinho was born in Setúbal, Portugal, on 26 January 1963.

He has managed Benfica, União de Leiria, Porto, Chelsea, Internazionale. He once acted as an interpreter for Bobby Robson, working with him at top Portuguese teams Sporting Clube de Portugal and FC Porto and the Spanish FC Barcelona.

Known for his outspokenness but popular with his fans, peers and the press.

He was named the world's best football manager by the International Federation of Football History and Statistics for the 2004-5 and the 2005-6 seasons.

Mourinho was arrested in the UK in 2007 for obstructing police who had attempted to put his dog into quarantine.

~

"If I made a mistake then I apologise. I am happy that I'm not going to jail because of that"
José Mourinho

"There is no pressure at the top. The pressure's being second or third"
José Mourinho

"We are on top at the moment but not because of the club's financial power. We are in contention for a lot of trophies because of my hard work"
José Mourinho

"You can have the top stars to bring the attention, you can have the best stadium, you can have the best facilities, you can have the most beautiful project in terms of marketing and all this kind of thing. But if you don't win... all the work these people are doing is forgotten"
José Mourinho

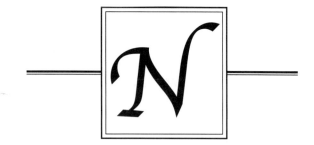

"It's a case of putting all our eggs into the next ninety minutes"
Phil Neal

"The run of the ball is not in our court at the moment"
Phil Neal

"I'm not superstitious or anything like that, but I'll just hope we'll play our best and put it in the lap of the gods"
Terry Neill

"Football today, it's like a game of chess. It's all about money"
Newcastle United fan, Radio 5 Live

"Carragher's played five hundred games in eleven years. That's nearly fifty games a year"
Mike Newell

Own Goals!

"Tell the Kraut to get his ass up front. We don't pay a million for a guy to hang around in defence"
NY Cosmos executive on Beckenbauer's positioning

"Paul Jewell's sides are always hard to break down, although Manchester United have a habit of breaking his sides down pretty easily"
Charlie Nicholas

"The ball's in so much pain, I can hear it screaming"
Charlie Nicholas

"It was a continuance of what we have seen most of the season – that is, various clubs beating each other"
Ron Noades

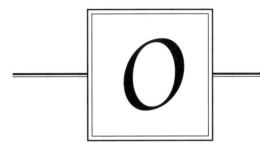

Own Goals!

"I was a young lad when I was growing up"
David O'Leary

"He lacks that confidence which he possesses"
Martin O'Neill

"I don't want to pick out individuals but
Gareth Barry was immense, James Milner
had tremendous energy and Emile Heskey
was quite brilliant"
Martin O'Neill

"Neil Lennon wasn't sent off for scoring a goal,
and that's what annoys me"
Martin O'Neill

"The best thing for them to do is to stay at nil-nil
until they score the goal"
Martin O'Neill

Own Goals!

"Mind you, I've been here during the bad times
too – one year we came second"
Bob Paisley

"I said to the players before the start, 'Just go out
and give it 100%. I am not asking for any more
than that'"
Carlton Palmer

"Obviously it would be tough playing up in the
Premiership next season, but I wouldn't lose any
sleepless nights"
Alan Pardew

"The offside flag went up immediately,
if not before"
Jonathan Park

"Celtic were at one time nine points ahead,
but somewhere along the road, their ship went
off the rails"
Richard Park

Alan Parry (b.1948)

Sports commentator.

Alan Parry was born in Garston, Liverpool, England, in 1948.

He is a British sports commentator concentrating mainly on football and athletics. He has commentated for the BBC, ITV and Sky as well as for BBC and commercial radio (covering the 1976, 1980 and 1984 summer Olympics and from 1981 commentating on *Match of the Day*, both for the BBC).

He is a famous Liverpool supporter.

"And Ritchie has now scored eleven goals, exactly double the number he scored last season"
Alan Parry

Own Goals!

"He hit that one like an arrow"
Alan Parry

"He's scored! There's no end to the stoppage of this drama"
Alan Parry

"The ball was literally glued to the back of his foot – into the back of the net"
Alan Parry

"The Liverpool players are passing the cup down the line like a new born baby. Although, when they are back in the dressing room they will probably fill it with Champagne, something you should never do to a baby"
Alan Parry

"2-0 is a cricket score in Italy"
Alan Parry

"I can see the carrot at the end of the tunnel"
Stuart Pearce

"David [Johnson] has scored sixty-two goals in one hundred and forty-eight games for Ipswich and those statistics tell me that he plays games and scores goals"
David Platt

"A game is not won until it is lost"
David Pleat

"And the steam has gone completely out of the Spanish sails"
David Pleat

"He's got a brain under his hair"
David Pleat

"I was inbred into the game by my father"
David Pleat

Own Goals!

"Pires has got something about him, he can go
both ways depending on who's facing him"
David Pleat

"That would have put the icing on his start"
David Pleat

"They are the victims of their own downfall"
David Pleat

"This is a real cat and carrot situation"
David Pleat

"We just ran out of legs"
David Pleat

"Winning isn't the end of the world"
David Pleat

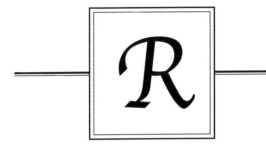

Own Goals!

"It's now 1-1, an exact reversal of the score on
Saturday"
Radio 5 Live

"The score is Sunderland nil, Leicester nil, the
temperature is nil and the entertainment value
is not much above nil"
Radio 5 Live

"It's headed away by John Clark, using his head"
Derek Rae

"There is great harmonium in the dressing room"
Alf Ramsey

"In football, if you stand still you go backwards"
Peter Reid

Harry Redknapp (b.1947)

Football manager and former player.

Henry James Redknapp was born in London, England, on 2 March 1947.

He played for West Ham United, Bournemouth, Brentford, and Seattle Sounders before managing Bournemouth, West Ham United, Portsmouth, Southampton and Tottenham Hotspur.

While in his second spell at Portsmouth, he managed the side to win the 2008 FA Cup. This was his first and so far only major trophy as a player or manager.

Popular with fans. Accused of corruption by the British Press.

His son, Jamie Redknapp, played under him at Bournemouth and at Southampton. He is also uncle to Chelsea player Frank Lampard, who played under him at West Ham United.

~

"By the look of him he must have headed a lot
of balls"
Harry Redknapp

"Dani is so good-looking I don't know whether
to play him or f*ck him"
Harry Redknapp

"Even when they had Moore, Hurst and Peters,
West Ham's average finish was about
seventeenth. It just shows how crap the other
eight of us were"
Harry Redknapp

"Hartson's got more previous than Jack the Ripper"
Harry Redknapp

"Samassi Abou don't speak the English too good"
Harry Redknapp

"There's only one way Newcastle can go and
that's up. But they can go down as well"
Harry Redknapp

"With the foreign players it's more difficult. Most
of them don't even bother with the golf, they
don't want to go racing. They don't even drink"
Harry Redknapp

"There are some big name players here like
Jimmy Floyd Hasselbaink"
Jamie Redknapp

"If you don't want to know the result, look away
now as we show you Tony Adams lifting the cup
for Arsenal"
Steve Rider

"We threw our dice into the ring and
turned up trumps"
Bruce Rioch

Bobby Robson (1933-2009)

Football manager and player.

Robert William Robson was born in Sacriston, England, on 18 February 1933 and died on 31 July 2009.

His professional playing career spanned nearly 20 years, during which time he played for Fulham, West Bromwich Albion, and, briefly, Vancouver Royals. He also played for the England national team.

After his playing career he found success as both a club and international manager, winning League Championships in both the Netherlands and Portugal, earning trophies in England and Spain, and taking England to the semi-final of the 1990 World Cup. He managed Fulham, Ipswich Town, the England national team, PSV Eindhoven, Sporting CP, Porto, Barcelona, and Newcastle United. His last management role was as a mentor to the manager of the Irish national football team.

Robson was awarded a CBE in 1990, created a Knight Bachelor in 2002, was inducted into England's National Football Museum's Hall of Fame in 2003 and into the special European Hall of Fame in 2008, and was the honorary president of Ipswich Town.

From 1991 onwards he suffered recurrent medical problems with cancer, and in March 2008 put his name and efforts into the Sir Bobby Robson Foundation, a cancer research charity. In August 2008, his lung cancer was confirmed to be terminal. He said: "My condition is described as static and has not altered since my last bout of chemotherapy... I am going to die sooner rather than later. But then everyone has to go sometime and I have enjoyed every minute". He died just under a year later.

≈

"Anything from 1-0 to 2-0 would be a nice result"
Bobby Robson

Own Goals!

"Eighteen months ago they [Sweden] were arguably one of the best three teams in Europe, and that would include Germany, Holland, Russia and anybody else if you like"
Bobby Robson

"Everyone's got tough games coming up. Manchester United have got Arsenal, Arsenal have got Manchester United and Leeds have got Leeds"
Bobby Robson

"Gary Speed has never played better, never looked fitter, never been older"
Bobby Robson

"He's got his legs back, of course, or his leg – he's always had one but now he's got two"
Bobby Robson

"He's very fast and if he gets a yard ahead of himself nobody will catch him"
Bobby Robson

"He's not the Carl Cort that we know he is"
Bobby Robson

"Home advantage gives you an advantage"
Bobby Robson

"His influence on the team through his personality and playing ability cannot be underestimated"
Bobby Robson

"If we start counting our chickens before they hatch, they won't lay any eggs in the basket"
Bobby Robson

"I'm not going to look beyond the semi-final... but I would love to lead Newcastle out at the final"
Bobby Robson

"In a year's time, he's a year older"
Bobby Robson

Own Goals!

"The margin is very marginal"
Bobby Robson

"I thought that individually and as a pair, they'd
do better together"
Bobby Robson

"Jermaine Jenas is a fit lad. He gets from box to
box in all of ninety minutes"
Bobby Robson

"Some of the goals were good, some of the goals
were sceptical"
Bobby Robson

"The first ninety minutes are the most important"
Bobby Robson

"Their football was exceptionally good – and
they played some good football"
Bobby Robson

"They can't change any of their players,
but they have changed one of their players and
that's the coach"
Bobby Robson

"We've got nothing to lose, and there's no point
losing this game"
Bobby Robson

"Where do you get an experienced player like
him with a left foot and a head?"
Bobby Robson

"It wasn't going to be our day on the night"
Bryan Robson

Own Goals!

"Paolo di Canio is capable of scoring the goal
he scored"
Bryan Robson

"It's a bit easier after that win over Newcastle.
That's a result that takes us that little bit further
from safety"
Bryan Robson

"We're going to start the game at nil-nil and go
out and try to get some goals"
Bryan Robson

"I think Manchester United is the biggest thing
in Manchester, and then after that it's
Coronation Street"
Cristiano Ronaldo

"We lost because we didn't win"
Cristiano Ronaldo

"Hagi is a brilliant player, but we're not going to get psychedelic over him"
Andy Roxburgh

"I don't blame individuals, I blame myself"
Joe Royle

"I don't make promises, I promise results"
Joe Royle

"If it had gone in, it would have been a goal"
Joe Royle

"I've seen players sent off for worse than that"
Joe Royle

"Of their goals, two came from headers and one was a header"
Joe Royle

"Our goalkeeper didn't have a save to make in ninety minutes, and yet he still ended up conceding four goals"
Joe Royle

"That was clearly a tackle aimed at getting revenge – or maybe it was just out-and-out retribution"
Joe Royle

"The Italians can blame no-one but themselves. They can blame the referee, but they can blame no-one but themselves"
Joe Royle

"We played well for the first ninety minutes"
Joe Royle

S

Own Goals!

"Whenever you leave Manchester United,
it's a step down. But Everton was a really good
step down"
Louis Saha

"Whoever invented football should be
worshipped as a God"
Hugo Sanchez

"I told Zola, 'I'm going to tell the truth about you
and let everyone know what a sneaky, horrible,
little man you are.' He replied, 'That's fine by me.
When I write my book, I'm going to say that you
look at me in the showers'"
Graeme Le Saux

"When I broke down on the motorway, everyone
was driving past me, giving me 'V' signs and
wanker signs. Even old men and women. I'm
hated, absolutely hated. But you've got to laugh"
Robbie Savage

"Stephen Bywater wants to be a cage fighter.
The only trouble is, his wife calls him her little
tunky-wunky"
Robbie Savage

"We had some bad experiences flying with
Blackburn. On one occasion, one of the lads
actually wet himself"
Robbie Savage

"I wouldn't be surprised if this game went
all the way to the finish"
Ian St. John

"In Latin America the border between soccer and
politics is vague. There is a long list of
governments that have fallen or been overthrown
after the defeat of the national team"
Luis Suarez

Bill Shankly (1913-1981)

Football manager and player.

William Shankly was born in Glenbuck, Scotland, on 2 September 1913 and died on 29 September 1981.

One of Britain's most famous, successful and respected football managers, Shankly was also a fine player whose career was interrupted by World War II. He played nearly 300 times in the Football League for Preston North End and represented Scotland in the national team.

He is most remembered, however, for his achievements as a manager, particularly with Liverpool. Shankly established Liverpool, which had been a Second Division club when he arrived, as one of the major forces in the English game. The club won three League Championships, two FA Cups and the UEFA Cup under Shankly, before his surprise retirement after the 1974 FA Cup Final. In all he managed Carlisle United, Grimsby Town, Workington, Huddersfield Town, and Liverpool.

Shankly was awarded an OBE in 1974.

He was inducted into England's National Football Museum's Hall of Fame in 2002.

He suffered a heart attack on 26 September 1981 and, although he survived this, his condition deteriorated and he died in Broadgreen Hospital in Liverpool on 29 September. After his cremation, his ashes were buried at Anfield Crematorium.

≈

"Some people believe football is a matter of life and death. I am very disappointed with that attitude. I can assure you it is much, much more important than that"
Bill Shankly

"At a football club, there's a holy trinity – the players, the manager and the supporters. Directors don't come into it. They are only there to sign the cheques"
Bill Shankly

Own Goals!

"If Everton were playing at the bottom of the
garden, I'd pull the curtains"
Bill Shankly

"If you are first, you are first. If you are second,
you are nothing"
Bill Shankly

"If you can't make decisions in life, you're a bloody
menace. You'd be better becoming an MP!"
Bill Shankly

"It's great grass at Anfield, professional grass!"
Bill Shankly

"Of course I didn't take my wife to see Rochdale
as an anniversary present, it was her birthday.
Would I have got married in the football season?
Anyway, it was Rochdale reserves"
Bill Shankly

"The difference between Everton and the Queen
Mary is that Everton carry more passengers!"
Bill Shankly

"There are two great teams on Merseyside:
Liverpool and Liverpool Reserves"
Bill Shankly

"With him in defence, we could play Arthur
Askey in goal"
Bill Shankly

"Yes Roger Hunt misses a few, but he gets in the
right place to miss them"
Bill Shankly

"If it comes to penalties, one of these two great
sides could go out on the whim of a ball"
Peter Shreeves

"There are 0-0's and 0-0's – and this was 0-0"
John Sillett

"The sight of opposing fans walking together
down Wembley Way – you won't get that
anywhere other than Wembley"
John Sillett

"From that moment the pendulum went
into reverse"
Gerald Sindstat

"One of Asa's great qualities is not scoring goals"
Roy Small

"Don't forget this club nearly went out of
extinction last year"
Alan Smith

"We had enough chances to win this game.
In fact, we did win"
Alex Smith

"He's captain of Rangers, and that's one of the
reasons he's captain"
Walter Smith

"If we'd won, it would have meant an historic
double-treble. But we weren't even thinking
about that"
Walter Smith

"Our goal scoring is like ketchup, you never now
how much is going to come out of the bottle"
Trond Sollied

"Of the ten sendings off, nine have been
different players, so it proves we're unlucky"
Keith Stevens

Own Goals!

"Anybody who plays for me should be a bad loser"
Graeme Souness

"If Liverpool fans had a choice of the Premier League or the Champions League, they'd take the Premier League. Or maybe both"
Graeme Souness

"Today's top players only want to play in London or for Manchester United. That's what happened when I tried to sign Alan Shearer and he went to Blackburn"
Graeme Souness

"Unless you like feeling someone you can't be a defender"
Graeme Souness

"Without picking out anyone in particular, I thought Mark Wright was tremendous"
Graeme Souness

"If you don't believe you can win, there is no point in getting out of bed at the end of the day"
Neville Southall

"Why didn't you just belt it, son?"
Gareth Southgate's mother

"We've got to get out there and set our stool out early"
Keith Stevens

"Alan McInally never broke a metatarsal in his career. Matt Le Tissier never broke sweat in his"
Jeff Stelling

"Cristiano Ronaldo wrote off his two-day old Ferrari. Thank goodness it wasn't a new one!"
Jeff Stelling

"I hear Stuart Kettlewell's been sent off for
violent conduct. He probably boiled over"
Jeff Stelling

"I've just heard the Reading coach has broken
down. Let's hope Wally Downes gets well soon"
Jeff Stelling

"Les Ferdinand said it's important that
Pavlyuchenko embraces the language. We feel
the same way about Paul Merson"
Jeff Stelling

"Santa Cruz has an escape clause in his contract.
A Santa Clause, you might call it"
Jeff Stelling

"The Scottish Cup sponsor is William Haughey,
whose made millions from refrigeration. So you
could say he's a fridge magnate"
Jeff Stelling

"The Glaswegian definition of an atheist: a bloke who goes to a Rangers-Celtic match to watch the football"
Sandy Strang

"Celtic against Arsenal isn't an even game. Arsene Wenger's got a machine gun while Tony Mowbray's got a water pistol"
Gordon Strachan

Although we are playing Russian roulette we are obviously playing Catch-22 at the moment and it's a difficult scenario to get my head round"
Paul Sturrock

"When a player makes a mistake, you get a yellow card, a suspension or a fine. When a professional referee does it, nothing happens. They can go home, sit down on the couch and scratch their balls!"
Michael Svensson

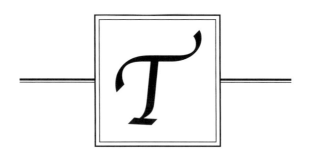

"David Beckham literally said, 'Pick me or if you're not going to, then don't pick me'"
Graham Taylor

"I'd never allow myself to let myself call myself a coward"
Graham Taylor

"In football, time and space are the same thing"
Graham Taylor

"It's a game we've got to win. It's also a game we've not got to lose"
Graham Taylor

"It's the only way we can lose, irrespective of the result"
Graham Taylor

"People always remember the second half"
Graham Taylor

"Shearer could be at 100% fitness, but not peak fitness"
Graham Taylor

"To be really happy, we must throw our hearts over the bar and hope that our bodies will follow"
Graham Taylor

"Very few of us have any idea whatsoever of what life is like living in a goldfish bowl – except, of course, for those of us who are goldfish"
Graham Taylor

"He was a no risk-free signing"
Stan Ternent

"It was caviar and cabbage stuff"
Phil Thompson

"At matches, I used to get abuse about my weight
and big nose. And that was just from my family"
Matt Le Tissier

"There's been no chances in the game, but
Wolves had the first chance"
Matt Le Tissier

"I am often interested in players but I never say
so, although I am looking for a striker and a
midfield player"
Colin Todd

"If the players want to make it hard for me, I am
happy to make it twice as hard for them"
Wendy Toms, the first female referee

"Drogba was having it off under Phil Scolari"
Phil Thompson

"Sirvet was literally – literally – up Koller's backside!"
Andy Townsend

"I've told the players we need to win so that I can have the cash to buy some new ones"
Chris Turner

"... and tonight we have the added ingredient of Kenny Dalglish not being here"
Martin Tyler

"He had an eternity to play that ball... but he took too long over it"
Martin Tyler

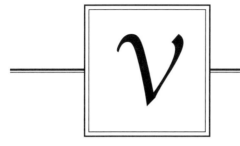

Terry Venables (b.1943)

Football manager and former player.

Known as "El Tel". Terence Frederick Venables was born in London, England, on 6 January 1943.

He played for Chelsea, Tottenham Hotspur, Queen's Park Rangers, Crystal Palace, St Patrick's Athletic and the England national team before managing such teams as Crystal Palace, Queen's Park Rangers, Barcelona, and Tottenham Hotspur.

He was inducted into England's National Football Museum's Hall of Fame in 2007.

Venables is a man of many talents: a one-time novelist, dramatist, big-band singer and mime artist..! Also founder of the Terry Venables School of Soccer.

Voted Coach of the Year (for Barcelona), 1984-5, by *World Soccer Magazine*.

∼

"Apart from their goals, Norway haven't scored"
Terry Venables

"Certain people are for me and certain people
are pro me"
Terry Venables

"Everybody says Steve McManaman played on
the left for me in Euro 96 but he never played on
the left. The one time he did play on the left was
against Switzerland"
Terry Venables

"If history is going to repeat itself I should think
we can expect the same thing again"
Terry Venables

"I felt a lump in my mouth as the ball went in"
Terry Venables

Own Goals!

"If you can't stand the heat in the dressing-room, get out of the kitchen"
Terry Venables

"If you can't outplay the opposition, you must outnumber them"
Terry Venables

Jimmy Hill: "Don't sit on the fence, Terry, what chance do you think Germany has got of getting through?"
Terry Venables: "I think it's fifty–fifty"

"It may have been going wide, but nevertheless it was a great shot on target"
Terry Venables

"It was never part of our plans not to play well, it just happened that way"
Terry Venables

"I've been asked that question for the last six months. It is not fair to expect me to make such a fast decision on something that has been put upon me like that"
Terry Venables

"The mere fact that he's injured stops him getting injured again, if you know what I mean"
Terry Venables

"They didn't change positions, they just moved the players around"
Terry Venables

"There are two ways of getting the ball. One is from your own team-mates, and that's the only way"
Terry Venables

"The spirit he has shown has been second to none"
Terry Venables on Terry Fenwick's drink-driving charge

Own Goals!

"When you make a mistake, that becomes
a mistake"
Terry Venables

"At the start of the season you're strong enough
to win the Premiership and the European Cup,
but you have to be as strong in March, when the
fish are down"
Gianluca Vialli

"When Manchester United are at their best I am
close to orgasm"
Gianluca Vialli

"I once missed an open goal live on TV. Although
it was a hard open goal"
Rowan Vine

"It's been hard being out for a year with a broken
leg. But everyone's kept me on my toes"
Rowan Vine

"If I walked on water, my accusers would say it is
because I can't swim"
Berti Vogts

"I do like a nice sock on my foot"
Moritz Volz

"I wear these things called toe condoms, which
are little jelly slips that go over your toes"
Moritz Volz

"One time I experimented with a woman's hair
removal machine"
Moritz Volz

"The black cod might be lovely to eat but it's a
seriously ugly fish. The Peter Beardsley of the
sea. Not like me, Moritz rainbow trout Volz"
Moritz Volz

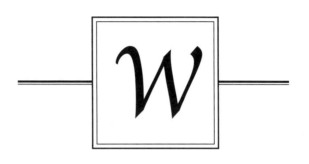

"I just wonder what would have happened if the shirt had been on the other foot"
Mike Walker

"It will be a cracking match and a close one – maybe decided by a referee's decision, an odd bounce or something like an over-the-line goal"
Neil Warnock

"Matches don't come any bigger than FA Cup quarter-finals"
Neil Warnock

"We were unanimous – well, you two were"
Elton Welsby

"And that's Aston Villa's first league goal since their last one"
Elton Welsby

Own Goals!

"As long as no-one scored, it was always going to be close"
Arsene Wenger

"Davor has a left leg and a nose in the box"
Arsene Wenger

"He made the impossible possible"
Arsene Wenger

"Of the nine red cards this season we probably deserved half of them"
Arsene Wenger

"The only thing I have in common with George Best is that we come from the same place, play for the same club and were discovered by the same man"
Norman Whiteside

The world's funniest football quotes

"We keep kicking ourselves in the foot"
Ray Wilkins

"As one door closes, another one shuts"
Howard Wilkinson

"We have to roll up our sleeves and get our
knees dirty"
Howard Wilkinson

"I'm a firm believer that if the other side scores
first you have to score twice to win"
Howard Wilkinson

"If they hadn't scored, we would've won"
Howard Wilkinson

Dean Windass (b.1969)

Footballer (retired from playing in October 2009).

Dean Windass was born in Kingston upon Hull, England, on 1 April 1969.

He played for Hull City, North Ferriby United, Aberdeen, Oxford United, Bradford City, Middlesbrough, Sheffield United, and Darlington. A Hull City legend in every possible sense, in 2008 Windass scored the fantastic goal that took Hull City up to the Premiership for the first time in their history. He also scored his last Premier League goal at the age of 39, becoming Hull City's oldest ever scorer.

A popular but somewhat controversial player, Windass was once given a red card three times in one game!

Windass' autobiography, *Deano – From Gipsyville to the Premiership*, was published in 2007.

$\sim$

"I'd like to put all these rumours to rest once and for all. I'm not off to Real Madrid. I'm going to Benidorm – same as last year"
Dean Windass

"I have a simple motto for dealing with pressure: win or lose, I always booze"
Dean Windass

"I've got my own strip pre-season regime. First thing in the morning I have a light workout by turning the pages of the paper, then I build up my thumb muscles by turning on the box and flicking through the channels"
Dean Windass

"On the Continent diving is known as simulation while we call it being a fanny"
Dean Windass

"QPR's owner looks like Peter Stringfellow at the
end of a night out"
Dean Windass

"Robinho was apparently crying his eyes out
and begging to leave Spain. I know how he felt.
I've had a few holidays like that"
Dean Windass

"The adrenalin rush after scoring was incredible.
Imagine leaping off the wing of a jet fighter into
a lake of Champagne while having the best shag
of your life. Well, it was ten thousand times
better than that!"
Dean Windass

"The real reason Ronaldo wants to leave is he
knows he's gonna be mauled by yours truly –
Yorkshire's finest"
Dean Windass

"To be a manager you need skin as thick as an elephant's foreskin"
Dean Windass

"We're doing high altitude training in the Alps which should be a good chance to practise my yodelling"
Dean Windass

"It's sod's law. Now I've got time to improve my golf it's the wrong time of year"
Howard Wilkinson

"We are not putting our cape over the tunnel: we are putting our cape in the tunnel"
Howard Wilkinson

"There were a few thousand people behind that goal sucking like mad"
Steve Wilson

Own Goals!

"Both sides have scored a couple of goals, and both sides have conceded a couple of goals"
Peter Withe

"The rules of soccer are very simple, basically it is this: If it moves, kick it. If it doesn't move, kick it until it does"
Phil Woosnam

"It took a lot of bottle for Tony Adams to own up"
Ian Wright on the Arsenal captain's confession to alcoholism

"Without being too harsh on David Beckham, he cost us the match"
Ian Wright

"I don't really believe in targets, because my next target is to beat Stoke City"
Ron Wylie

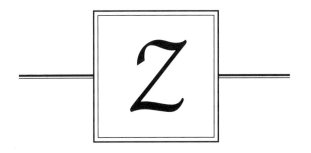

Own Goals!

"We have faced African teams, we have faced English teams – so we are ready to face Scotland because we know what their play will be like"
Mario Zagallo

"Tony Blair was on *Football Focus* the other week and named me as one of his favourite players. My father-in-law phoned me and said 'I've never heard such rubbish!' - but I think it's great. I voted Lib-Dem last time but I'm Labour again now"
Arjan De Zeeuw